My War
LAND GIRL

Philip Steele

HODDER
Wayland

an imprint of Hodder Children's Books

Produced for Hodder Wayland by
Discovery Books Ltd
Unit 3, 37 Watling Street, Leintwardine, Shropshire SY7 0LW

First published in 2003 by Hodder Wayland, an imprint of Hodder Children's Books

British Library Cataloguing in Publication Data
Steele, Philip, 1948-
    Land girl. - (My war)
    1.Women's Land Army 2.World War, 1939-1945 - War work -
    Great Britain - Juvenile Literature 3.World War, 1939-1945 - Women
    - Great Britain - Juvenile literature - 4. Great Britain - History -
    George VI, 1936-1952 - Juvenile literature
    I. Title II.Williams, Gianna
    941'.084'082

    ISBN 0 7502 4217 5

Printed and bound in Hong Kong

Series editor: Gianna Williams
Designer: Ian Winton
Picture research: Rachel Tisdale

Hodder Children's Books would like to thank the following for the loan of their material:
Beamish: p. 24; Hulton Getty: *cover* (carrying hay), pp. 7, 8, 10, 12, 13, 15, 16 (bottom), 17 (bottom),
19, 20, 21, 22 (bottom), 23 (bottom); Imperial War Museum: p. 18; Robert Opie Collection: pp. 6, 14,
23 (top).

Discovery Books would also like to thank the following for the kind loan of their material: Bill
Scolding/Serpentine Design, Arthur M Procter/AM Photographics, Jean Procter MBE, Margaret Rayner,
Elsie Hendy, Pat Coggon, Doreen Jones and the British WLA Society.

Hodder Children's Books
A division of Hodder Headline Limited
338 Euston Road
London NW1 3BH

Contents

The 'Land Girls'

In 1939 the United Kingdom was on the brink of war with Germany. Everyone hoped for peace, but many people felt that they should prepare for the worst. The government decided to organize a Women's Land Army (WLA). Its aim was not to fight, but to work on the land, producing food and timber. In this book, five women who served with the WLA as 'land girls' tell us what their lives were like during the Second World War of 1939 to 1945.

ELSIE HENDY and PAT COGGON

Elsie (above) and Pat (below) were Londoners. Elsie, born in 1925, was from Wandsworth, and Pat, born in 1926, was from Tooting. Both served in Cornwall, where they became good friends.

JEAN PROCTER

Jean was born in Lancashire in 1919, but moved to Edinburgh when she was 17, as her father was Scottish. She worked in Cheshire as a land girl.

MARGARET RAYNER

Margaret, born in 1925, was born at Blaydon, on the River Tyne. She spent the war years working in a sawmill in Worcester.

DOREEN JONES

Doreen was also born in 1925, the daughter of a lighthouse-keeper. She spent most of her childhood in South Wales and served there as a land girl, too.

The Women's Land Army

The Women's Land Army (WLA) had first been set up in 1917, during the First World War. In June 1939 the government brought it back into being, two months before war was declared. There was one WLA organization for England and Wales, another for Scotland.

▲ The WLA launched a poster campaign to recruit women aged between 18 and 40.

JEAN

I joined up with the Women's Land Army in January 1939. I had to travel down to Coventry, in Warwickshire, to register. Then war broke out, and we were all re-organized. I was number 28900.

Women were needed to work in farming for several reasons. Men who had worked on the land were now needed to fight in the army. At the same time, more and more food needed to be produced in Britain. Ships which had imported food before the war now risked enemy attack.

Back to the land,
We must all lend a hand,
To the farms and the
fields we must go.
There's a job to be done,
Though we can't fire a
gun
We can still do our bit
with a hoe...

▲ This was part of the official Land Army Song, written and composed by land girls.

◀ A uniformed land girl explains the work of the WLA at a recruitment stand set up in a store in Oxford Street, London.

At the outbreak of war there were 1,000 land girls. By 1943 there were 87,000 of them. Forestry workers in the WLA were organized into a separate Timber Corps in 1942.

MARGARET

Why did I join the Timber Corps? I wanted to help out and I looked forward to a change of scene. They sent me from Tyneside to Worcester. I really was ready for anything!

A New Way of Life

Some new land girls were leaving their families for the first time. As the train carried them to their new homes, many felt anxious, but excited.

Some were put to work in areas they already knew, but others had to travel to places which were very different from their homes. Women from big cities had to learn about life in the countryside.

▼ Women who had only worked in offices or shops now had to do hard, physical labour in all weathers.

ELSIE

I travelled down to Cornwall by train. I had to sit in the corridor, because the carriages were packed with sailors bound for ships docked at Plymouth, in Devon. It was damp and misty when I arrived at Gwinear Road station. Real Cornish weather! It was all so quiet after London....

Young women were now doing work that was usually done by men. At first many farmers and foresters did not believe that they were up to the job. They soon changed their minds. Most of the new recruits worked hard and well.

JEAN

I worked at different farms, up to three at the same time. It wasn't always easy at first. Some farmers missed their sons working on the farm, and some farmers' wives were suspicious and jealous of the new arrivals.

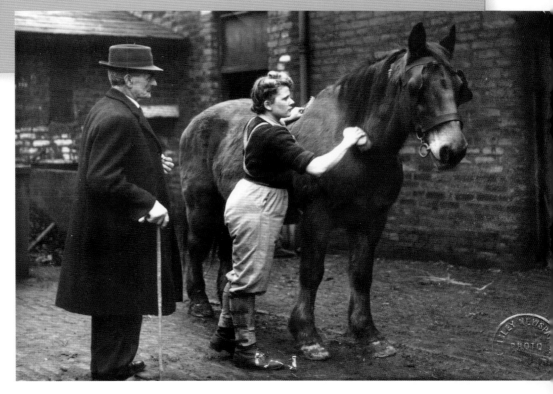

▶ After they had been trained in farm work, women were given tests of their ability. Here Jean shows the examiner she can groom a horse.

MARGARET

Suddenly here I was, a 17 year-old shorthand-typist, in a completely different world – a busy sawmill. Everyone made us very welcome, they were so kind. Other women were already employed in the wood-turning shop, so I didn't feel too out of place.

After a month's training, land girls were paid 28 shillings (£1.40) for a 48-hour week (50 in summer). By 1944 the rate had gone up by £1.

Home from Home

Land girls often worked on several different farms, sometimes as a team. Some stayed with their own family or relatives, but many shared 'digs' (lodgings) with other WLA members.

◀ This photo shows land girls coming off a shift at the end of the day. Living and working with other women was a new experience for most land girls. They had to learn how to get on with each other.

PAT

ELSIE

Many people offered accommodation for the land girls. We shared digs in a bungalow owned by a Miss Gilbert. She was aged about 60 and was very prim, proper and precise. We had to be back early in the evenings. She would really give us a telling off if it was after 10 o'clock. But it was a wonderful home for us there, really.

The WLA took over many buildings and used them as hostels. These varied from castles and lovely old houses to former sports pavilions and even converted chicken houses.

MARGARET

I shared digs with four other women, all in the Timber Corps. That was quite a common arrangement. It was easier to arrange our work that way, and to make friends.

▲ Jean used a bike to travel to work and to get around on the farm.

Many women stayed in farmhouses and farm cottages. In the 1940s there were few luxuries, especially in remote countryside areas. Some farms still had no running water, no electricity supply and no indoor toilets.

DOREEN

I started off as part of a mobile group, based in Cardiff. We were taken out to different farms each day. Then I was sent to the Gower, near Swansea. We were put up in one old house that was meant to be haunted. I didn't see any ghosts, though!

Getting the Kit

The Women's Land Army had an official uniform. It included a broad-brimmed brown felt hat, a light cotton shirt, a green jumper and khaki-coloured breeches.

▶ Timber Corps workers, who were nicknamed 'lumberjills' (instead of 'lumberjacks') wore dungarees for felling trees in the forests.

JEAN

The clothes I got were much too big! I'm only 1.57 metres (5 foot 2 inches) tall and nothing fitted. It took ages for any wellies to come and then I got two left-footed ones. Luckily they were too big, so I just stuffed them with newspaper. In the end the owner of a local shoe shop complained on my behalf. He said it was disgraceful!

Women were also issued with working clothes, such as wellingtons or heavy boots and leggings, socks, coats, dungarees and oilskins. They often tied up their hair with a scarf to keep their hair clean, out of their eyes and, most importantly, out of farm machinery.

▼ Here Timber Corps women try on a new delivery of wellingtons, or 'gumboots' as they were called in those days.

MARGARET

The Timber Corps uniform was much the same as the WLA, only we had green berets with a badge showing a tree. In the sawmill we wore denim overalls, I remember. They were cream coloured.

▼ The WLA badge showed a wheat sheaf below a crown. Members were given flashes and armbands to show how long they had served.

With textiles such as cotton in short supply during the war, clothing was strictly rationed. You could only buy new clothes with special coupons issued by the government. Because WLA members were already issued with clothes, they were given fewer coupons.

▶ A land girl in Worcestershire carries two new-born lambs from the sheds. Cotton overalls were worn for most farm work.

13

Meals in Wartime

Food was in short supply during the war and was strictly rationed. Typical wartime foods included powdered eggs and powdered milk. There were no imported foods, such as bananas.

Oh, we did pretty well here in Cornwall. Real eggs twice a week! We had meat almost every day, veal or meat pies. Miss Gilbert would give us girls her share. We were certainly better off for food than our relatives back in London.

There was little eating out in wartime. The WLA wasn't part of the Services, so we couldn't use their canteens. Sometimes we land girls went into Manchester, to King George's Club. They served Sunday lunch and it cost one shilling and sixpence (8p).

► ▼ Wartime cookery books and posters did their best to make the most basic foods seem interesting.

The KITCHEN FRONT

122 WARTIME RECIPES broadcast by Frederick Grisewood, Mabel Constanduros and others, specially selected by the Ministry of Food.

6ᵈ

Shredded CABBAGE "makes" a salad!

In some country areas people did better than in towns. For example, some villagers kept a pig in the back garden and had it killed for bacon by a pig man that travelled from place to place.

The land girls needed a good diet to stay strong and healthy. Meals were basic, but most of them did get a cooked breakfast and a packed lunch or bread and cheese. Some farmers were a bit mean and begrudged the women even a cup of tea.

MARGARET

One day the River Severn flooded. We couldn't get back to our digs for lunch and were so hungry. Then some of the big timber lorries got through the water and one of the drivers gave me a sandwich. It had a whole lamb chop and two beetroots in it – a real feast!

◀ Strong tea is dished out to the Timber Corps from a milk churn, during a break from felling trees near Bury St Edmunds. Mugs of tea kept the lumberjills warm in winter and quenched their thirst in summer.

Farms and Market Gardens

The Women's Land Army took on every kind of farm work. Land girls dug ditches and laid hedges. They fed chickens, milked cows and learned to round up sheep with dogs. They ploughed the land, either with tractors or with the big shire-horses still used in those days. They built haystacks and at harvest time worked from dawn till dusk.

▲ Land girls with pitchforks and rakes bring in the hay in Essex. It all looks great fun, but it was very hard work.

JEAN

Bales of hay and wheat sheaves are hard to carry when you're little. I still have back problems today. Potato planting, that was another tricky job. You had to slot the seed potatoes through a moving belt and it was very easy to miss. One of the nastiest jobs was transporting lime. The dust made my nose bleed.

Much of the land girls' work was dangerous. Farm machinery was much less safe than it is today and accidents were common.

▶ Jean had to learn about using farm machinery. Here she is operating a corn drill.

▲ Some land girls learned greenhouse skills on the royal estate at Sandringham.

Over 10,000 land girls worked on market gardens, growing vegetables and fruit.

DOREEN

In the market gardens, I sometimes had to pick Brussels sprouts when they were coated with ice. My fingers were frozen stiff! When I worked on the farm, the really dangerous job was standing on top of the stack, feeding the thrashing machine. It could really have mangled you if you'd slipped!

Off the Farm

The Women's Land Army did not just organize work on the farms. Some worked in land reformation: draining bogs, for example, so that the soil could be used for farming.

Many land girls worked in pest control, destroying rats which were a threat to public health or killing off rabbits or moles which were damaging crops. Rat-catchers learned to use dangerous poisons such as zinc and arsenic.

JEAN

One incident still gives me nightmares. I met a huge rat down a big drain. It bared its yellow teeth! I had to kill it with a shovel, and everyone was shouting at me not to be scared.

◄ A land girl spreads rat poison on a fence. Pest control was not a popular job among land girls but was essential for the safety of people and the protection of crops.

MARGARET

I worked outside, under an awning. I operated a pendulum saw, which was 75 centimetres (30 inches) across. The saw had a guard on one side, but the open side was really dangerous. I came near to losing my fingers one day! Our sawmill produced handles for tools and brooms, tent pegs for the US Army and crosses for soldiers' graves.

ELSIE

I didn't like pest control very much! When a land girl left a nearby farm, I transferred to dairy work and did a milk round instead. That farm was where I met my future husband, Bill.

Timber Corps women felled big trees and trimmed off the branches. They learned to haul timber by horse and tractor, and went out with low-loader lorries. Many worked in sawmills. Timber was needed to make telegraph poles and pit-props in coalmines.

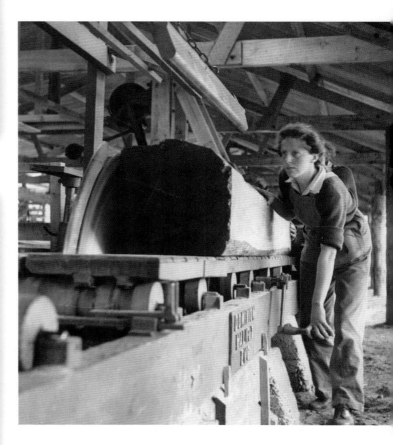

▲ Sawmill machinery was dangerous, and women had to pay attention every second. An accident could happen in an instant.

The Countryside at War

The land girls were less at risk than their friends who stayed in the cities. Bombing raids targeted docks or factories. Even so, in surrounding country areas there was always the risk of stray bombs, crashed aircraft or exploding ammunition dumps.

DOREEN

I did experience heavy bombing early on in the war, during the Swansea 'blitz'. But that was before I joined the Women's Land Army. Out in the countryside, things were quieter.

The countryside looked different in wartime. Road signs were removed, in case the enemy invaded. There were air-raid wardens in the villages, making sure that no lights were showing at night to guide enemy bombers. Many WLA members also took on extra work, such as watching for fires.

◀ Road signs are taken down in Surrey at the start of the war.

In some regions land girls were in real danger. In 1944, thousands of 'doodle-bugs' (flying bombs) came down on the farmland and villages of southeast England.

I did fire watch duty. The sawmill at Worcester was right by a petrol depot, so an air raid could have started a blaze. Luckily, it never happened.

◄ Farmland could also be used as an invasion route by the enemy. Many fields were covered with obstacles, such as these derelict cars, to prevent landing by aircraft.

JEAN

I joined NARPAC (the National Air-Raid Precaution for Animal Care) and learned how to do first aid for animals. I had to wear a tin hat for that job.

PAT

We were issued with gas masks, but they were awkward to carry and uncomfortable to wear. There was little risk of an attack, so we didn't wear them!

Free Time

The land girls worked so hard that they were often tired out by the time they got home. They did not have television in those days. Some had radios (which people then called the wireless), or records played on wind-up gramophones.

▲ News about the war could be heard on the 'wireless', or radio.

ELSIE

Dances? We never went to them much. They showed films, though, at the Mullion Institute (village hall) twice a week. There were newsreels and features. You had to pay extra for a cushion.

Some WLA members were not really looking for fun, but others loved to go out dancing when they could.

◀ Dances offered land girls a chance to forget about the mud and the aching muscles of the farmyard.

DOREEN

They had dances at the village hall. Mind you, it was a three or four mile walk just to get there!

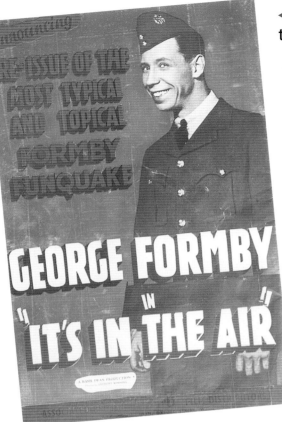

◀ One of the most popular British film stars was the comedian George Formby.

In some parts of the countryside there were airfields or army camps full of other young people, including British troops, Poles, Czechs and 'Yanks' (Americans).

Activities officially encouraged by the WLA included dances and whist drives (card games). Many hostels organized keep-fit and first aid classes.

JEAN

There wasn't much going on in the countryside round us. The land girls in our area, up to 42 of them, would get together for socials every now and then, just tea and sandwiches in the Guide hut. Sometimes we held a 'brains trust' (a discussion group) or a dance.

▲ At 'make-and-mend' classes (above) women learned how to make and alter clothes cheaply.

The End of the War

The Second World War lasted six years, but on 15 August 1945 it came to an end at last. There were wild celebrations and soon the troops were returning home.

▶ Peace at last! However, hardships and food shortages continued for many years after the war, and many land girls stayed on to help out.

MARGARET

When the war ended, the Timber Corps helped us find other jobs. I got clerical work in Worcester with the civil service – the War Department. Then I was transferred back to the northeast, to Darlington, which was where I got married.

The Timber Corps was disbanded as soon as the war was over. Some land girls carried on until 1950, when the Women's Land Army was finally stood down. Members were given careers advice, but unlike the troops they did not receive a final payment or issue of clothing.

Many land girls now got married and raised families. Some became full-time farmers, so the work they had learned in wartime proved very useful.

As the troops came home, many men returned to work on the land. However, women had proved beyond doubt that they could turn their hand to almost anything and do it well.

▶ Doreen (top right in 1943) was glad of her wartime experience, and she continued farming after the war.

Looking Back

All those who served with the Women's Land Army have strong memories of how their lives were changed. Many remember funny incidents and happy moments, and some have scary tales to tell as well.

PAT

We did have some fun. We shared an old car, called 'Black Bess'. Petrol was rationed, but we got by. One day Bess wouldn't start. The whole village came out to help. There was the butcher and the minister, all pushing....

ELSIE

Land girls agree that despite all the hardships, people stood by each other in those days. Life offered no luxuries, but it did offer a sense of purpose.

▶ Old photos bring back happy memories of wartime friendships for Pat and Elsie, shown here on the bonnet of 'Black Bess'.

DOREEN

We all had to do our bit. My brother was taken prisoner fighting in Crete. My sister worked for the NAAFI (the Services' clubs). And I served as a land girl.

◀ Jean is photographed hard at work repairing a hedge.

The war was tragic, but it had to be fought. Racism and thuggery, which the German leader Adolf Hitler wanted to spread around the world, had to be defeated. The Women's Land Army had played its part.

MARGARET

After the war I went to a cinema and saw a film of the death camp at Belsen. I wept. It made me realize what the war had been about and why we had served.

▲ Doreen's unit poses with farm workers. When the war started, farmers' trade unions had been against WLA labour. By 1945 they were asking the WLA to carry on its good work.

Keeping in Touch

Many former land girls kept in touch with each other after the war. However the work of the Women's Land Army was not officially recognized for many years. The armed forces march past the Cenotaph in London each November, but, until recently, ex-land girls were not allowed to take part.

▲ In 1999 Doreen Jones (second from right) met up with other former land girls for a WLA reunion at Pencoed Agricultural College, Bridgend.

In 1964 Jean Procter decided to bring together old friends for a reunion. This was the start of the British WLA Society. In 1969, 5,000 members filled London's Royal Albert Hall for the first ever national reunion. Former land girls living in other countries, such as Australia and New Zealand, have also organized reunions.

MARGARET

I lost touch with my Timber Corps friends in Worcester after the war, but I met many women through the WLA Society and made new friends.

ELSIE

I stayed in Cornwall after the war and got married. Pat went back to London, but she missed Cornwall and came back after five years. We have remained good friends ever since.

▼ A letter of thanks was later sent to former land girls from Queen Elizabeth II.

By this personal message I wish to express to you

Miss Elsie Winifred Leigh.

my appreciation of your loyal and devoted service as a member of the Women's Land Army from 14th. February 1944 to 31st. May 1946. Your unsparing efforts at a time when the victory of our cause depended on the utmost use of the resources of our land have earned for you the country's gratitude.

Elizabeth R

Jean was awarded an honour, the MBE, for her hard work. There is now a WLA memorial in Coventry Cathedral and in the year 2000 surviving WLA members joined the Cenotaph parade. The work of the land girls was recognized at last.

◄ Margaret Rayner (wearing medals, second left) and other friends from the WLA Society meet up in November 2000 in order to march past the Cenotaph.

Glossary

Air-raid warden an official responsible for public safety during wartime bombing.

Ammunition dump a storage area for explosives, shells, etc.

Awning a cover providing shelter for working outdoors.

Blitz a slang word used in Britain to mean 'heavy bombing'. It came from the German word Blitzkrieg ('lightning war'), which referred to modern high-speed warfare with tanks and planes.

Breeches short trousers fastened at the knee.

Cenotaph the national war memorial in Whitehall, London.

Coupons books of tickets issued by the government, allowing people to buy goods that were being rationed.

Death camps concentration camps built across Europe under the rule of Adolf Hitler, the German leader. In these, millions of Jews, gypsies (Roma) and political opponents were imprisoned, tortured, starved and murdered.

Digs lodgings, somewhere to stay.

Doodle-bugs a nickname for flying bombs, unmanned rockets launched against targets in Britain during the Second World War.

Flash a simple, coloured badge sewn onto a uniform, showing to which unit the wearer belongs.

Forestry workers people who work in forests. They cut down trees, process the timber, plant new trees and control or care for other plants and wildlife in the forest.

Gas mask a mask with a filter designed to protect the wearer from poison gas attacks.

Gramophone another word for a record-player.

Hostel an official home for WLA members, with accommodation for between 10 and 120 land girls.

Import to ship goods into the country from abroad.

Khaki a brown-green colour.

Land girl a nickname for any member of the Women's Land Army.

Land reformation making new land available for farming, by draining bogs for example.

Lime a chalky substance dug into poor soils to help crops grow.

Market gardening horticulture, the growing of fruit and vegetables.

MBE stands for Member of the Order of the British Empire.

Mobile group a gang of land girls who were taken out to different workplaces each day, as required.

NAAFI Navy, Army and Air Force Institutes. They ran stores, canteens and clubs for servicemen and women at home and overseas.

Newsreel a news review shown in the cinema. Before television, most cinemas showed newsreel film.

Oilskins waterproof jackets and trousers.

Pendulum saw a large circular saw mounted on a swinging frame.

Pit-prop a support, formerly made of wood, used to hold up the roof of a mine shaft.

Racism believing that one part of the human race is superior to another part. The Nazis who ruled Germany believed that Jews and gypsies (Roma) were inferior people.

Rationing laws brought in because of wartime shortages which limited the amount of goods one person could buy. Food, clothing, petrol and many other items were rationed.

Running water water from the mains supply, piped into the house with taps. Where there was no mains connected, water had to be pumped from a well.

Sawmill a place where tree trunks are sawn into lengths of timber.

Services the armed forces: Army, Navy and Air Force.

Shilling the type of money used in Britain at the time of the war. There were twenty shillings in one pound, and 12 pence in one shilling.

Stand down to release troops from duty, to disband a unit.

Thrashing or threshing to separate the grain from the stalk after it has been harvested.

Tin hat a simple metal helmet.

Trade union a workers' association, formed with the aim of protecting pay and working conditions.

Wireless the common word for 'radio' at the time of the Second World War.

Wood-turning using machines to make strips of timber into round poles.

Further Reading

Non-fiction

Cross, Vince, *The Blitz: the Diary of Edie Benson London 1940-41*, Scholastic Hippo, 2001.

Hunter, Rebecca, *Growing Up In the Forties*, Hodder Wayland, 2002.

Reynoldson, Fiona, *The Home Front: Women's War*, Hodder Wayland, 1991.

Robson, Pam, *All About the Second World War 1939-45*, Hodder Wayland, 1996.

South, Nigel, *Family Life: Second World War*, Hodder Wayland, 1998.

Fiction

Hayer, Rosemary, *The Fox in the Wood: A Wartime Adventure*, Anglia Young Books, 1995.

Swindells, Robert, *Hurricane Summer*, Mammoth 1997.

Swindells, Robert, *Roger's War*, Mammoth 1999.

Resources

Books

Sackville-West, Vita, *The Women's Land Army*, Imperial War Museum, 1997.

This edition includes a contemporary account of the WLA, documents, photographs, poetry by WLA members and an Introduction by Jean Procter MBE.

Places to Visit

Many local museums, county shows and rallies feature the tractors, shire-horses and agricultural machinery that would have been familiar to the WLA. The British WLA Society recommends the Yorkshire Museum of Farming, Murton Park.

The Imperial War Museum, London, is the best place to find out about life in Britain during the Second World War.

Index

Numbers in *italics* indicate photographs.